reading sand

western literature series

SELECTED DESERT POEMS, 1976–2000

william l. fox

reading sand

University of Nevada Press

Reno & Las Vegas

🌱 *This project is supported by funding from the National Endowment for the Arts.*

Western Literature Series
University of Nevada Press,
Reno, Nevada 89557 USA
Copyright © 1977, 1994, 1995, 1999, 2001, 2002
by William L. Fox
All rights reserved
Manufactured in the United States of America
Design by Carrie House
Library of Congress Cataloging-in-Publication Data
Fox, William L., 1949–
Reading sand : poems / William L. Fox.
p. cm. — (Western literature series)
ISBN 0-87417-498-8 (pbk. : alk. paper)
1. Great Basin—Poetry. I. Title. II. Series.
PS3556.O966 R43 2002
811'.54—dc21   2002000643
The paper used in this book meets the requirements of
American National Standard for Information Sciences—
Permanence of Paper for Printed Library Materials,
ANSI Z Z39.48–1984. Binding materials were selected
for strength and durability.

FIRST PRINTING
11 10 09 08 07 06 05 04 03 02
5 4 3 2 1

to the wind

contents

Sitting atop Sand Mountain in 1974, an isolated five-hundred-foot-high dune in north-central Nevada, I wrote "wind" on the bright ground with my finger. The word, a shadow in sand, was instantly erased by the wind itself. Though I had no illusion that I had caused this event, it made me wonder how to make poems about the desert that would be just as physical and immediate—what would such work look like? I began to write severely literal poems grounded in the landscape around me, and have been doing so ever since.

At times I hesitated even to call what I was doing poetry, as the texts seemed more like small performances, never more so than while crawling backward on my knees down the middle of a highway while writing the black words in the white lines of a highway on a black road in the middle of a white, snow-covered desert one winter.

Distracted by forays into experimental visual texts and lured away by essays and nonfiction, I continued nonetheless to write minimalist poems about the desert. At times, I think I am working on a single poem, one in which the parts of language evolve slowly into elements of the landscape. Participles turn into stones and entire lines of poetry are subsumed by Paleolithic shorelines and horizons. The repetitive exchange of words transforms into sticks picked up by a pack rat for its midden, which in turn comes to resemble architecture. All of it eventually becomes a matter of archeology as the sand, which in early poems first obscures the neon signs of *monody* (1976), by the new poems in *glass* buries the entire city.

The Great Basin, my home desert, encourages such recursive thoughts. Covering almost all of Nevada and western Utah, it is a deeply repetitive landscape of arid basins and high ranges that betrays the cycles of earth, fire, and water underlying it. The entire region continues to swell, uplifted from underneath and pushing apart Reno and Salt Lake City at opposite ends of the Basin. Nevada alone carries three hundred and sixteen mountain ranges, some of them over thirteen thousand feet in elevation, all separated from each other by valleys that can run over a hundred miles long by twenty wide. The basins and ranges tend north by south, massive wrinkles reflecting how the North American tectonic plate overrides the Pacific one. The bones of the land are naked here, and so is the syntax of the poetry.

No water runs out of the Great Basin, all of it falling inward either to sink beneath the ground or to evaporate. Forming its western rim is the two-mile-high Sierra Nevada, an escarpment of granite that casts a deep rain shadow over almost the entire Basin. This is the largest, highest, and coldest desert in America. Because the air is so devoid of humidity, there is little blurring of ridges thirty and forty miles away, confounding our sense of distance. Because the spectrum of color in the vegetation is so narrow, our expectations of atmospheric perspective, of a shift in color from a warm foreground to cool background, are distorted likewise.

The ground at our feet and the distant mountains are all that we see. Nowhere is there a familiar tree or building against which we can measure ourselves. The cognitive dissonance is severe. We don't know where we are. Traditional wisdom about being lost in the wilderness—follow water downstream until you reach civilization—does not often work here. Follow convention and you are likely to end up stranded in the middle of an alkali flat.

The only way to understand the enormous space of the Great Basin is to invest time in your experience of it. Slowly your eyes will adjust to the extended reach of vision, and your ears will become accustomed to hearing only the wind and your heartbeat. You will learn to read your way around, cutting across the grain of the land instead of following it in order to find your bearings.

The pages here incorporate more white space than usual; the distance between words is multiplied. The syntax is more often implied than stated, often cut through entirely. The poems make their turns from reality to metaphor, just as do more traditional ones, but the shift is often just a single stone rolling underfoot. If the poems are read too quickly, meaning fails to accumulate.

I wrote "wind"—and was amazed to find myself still doing so more than twenty-five years later in Los Angeles, where I edited this collection. The Santa Ana winds arrived from the Great Basin with their load of sand, depositing it under the windowsill and door-jamb. It appeared that my place would travel with me. Though I do not believe my words brought the sand, any more than they did the wind, apparently I would continue to live on the same page as the desert.

acknowledgments

monody was first published as a chapbook by Tom Person at Laughing Bear Press in 1977.

geograph appeared in 1994 from Bob Blesse's Black Rock Press at the University of Nevada.

"the inland sea" appeared as "the inland sea" and "the inland sea, again" in *no roses review* of Chicago during 1995. Both poems are from *One Wave Standing,* a collection published by La Alameda Press in 1998.

"Perforated Object" first appeared in the anthology *Etched in Stone,* published by the Black Rock Press at the University of Nevada, Reno in 2001, and edited by Bill Stobb and Dana Gioia.

"archaeologos," "new sand," "pack rats," "city," and "petroglyphs" were published by Scott Slovic in Volume 6.2 of *ISLE: Interdisciplinary Studies in Literature and Environment.*

My thanks to these editors, whose interest and faith in the work have been especially sustaining, to Arthur Sze for his help in shaping the final manuscript, and to Jayna Conkey for the cover image. My deepest appreciation goes to Tom Radko, who over many years encouraged and thus made possible this collection.

monody

In the desert one becomes other: one becomes the one who knows the weight of the sky and the thirst of the earth; the one who has learned to take account of his own solitude. Far from excluding us, the desert envelops us. We become the immensity of sand, just as we are the book when we write.

EDMOND JABÉS, *The Desert to the Book*

1.

part   sand
part   salt
part   cloud

all   white
all   white

2.

all   land
all   lake
all   sky

part   blue
part   blue

3.

all   sand
all   salt
all   cloud

part   land
part   lake
part   sky

all   blue
all   blue

4.

some   land
some   lake
some   sky

part   blue
part   white

5.

some   sand
some   salt
some   cloud

all   blue
all   white

6.

some   sand
some   salt
some   cloud

some   white
some   blue

white sand
blue lake

white sand
blue lake

white sand
blue lake

white sand
salt lake

white sand
blue salt

white sand
white salt

hard
water

hard
earth

dry
ice

1.

sky
line

snow
line

water
mark

salt
line

2.

snow
sand
and
cloud

wind
and

white
shadow

3.

sand	rock
point	point

point	black
blue	point

4.

on
line

in
sight

beside
the point

1.

red
sand

red
sun

neon
neon

white
sand

white
sun

neon
neon

2.

blue
sky

blue
sand

one
on

one
off

3.

black
night

black
night

red
on

red
off

blue
one

blue

1.

river
run

run
down

down
river

2.

ground
down

down
under

under
ground

round
river

2.

rain
sand

sand
grain

and
rain

sand
gain

3.

rain
and

salt
grain

and
salt
again

4.

rain
and
rain

sand
and
salt
again

1.

pin
point

point
blank

2.

south
to
south

sand
to
sand

east
to
east

peak
to
peak

3.

black
shadow

a
matter
of
time

a
matter
of
course

4.

track
to
track

to
back

5.

a

way

a

round

a

circle

of

sand

a

point

blank

line

6.

point

a

to

point

b

part

point

part

line

geograph

Listening to an extremely gradual musical process opens my ears to it, but it always extends further than I can hear, and that makes it interesting to listen to that musical process again. That area of gradual (completely controlled) musical process, where one hears the details of the sound moving out away from intentions, occurring for their own acoustical reasons, is it.

STEVE REICH

six parts

rust   in   the   street

rust   in   the   sand

glass   underfoot   and

rust   in   your   hand

sand   in   your   mouth

sand   in   your   eyes

rail   ties   and   rust

long   lines   in   the   dust

rails   in   the   sand

rails   over   glass

hot   beds   of   rust

long   lines   of   dust

hot   sand   and   wire

   barbs   in   the   rust

hot   sky   and   wire

   barbs   in   the   dust

hot   barbs   at   night

hot   wire   and   rust

hot   barbs   hold   tight

hot   hands   and   brush

wind   over   rust

wind   in   the   wire

wind   at   your   back

wind   and   white   dusk

leaving elko

along   the   ridge

all   snow   and   moon

west   wind   and   cloud

along   the   way

all   night   long

the   ridges   run

north   to   south

in   cold   and   cloud

light   first   comes

along   the   edge

and   my   tracks   run

from   night   to   day

along   the   ridge

all   day   one   cloud

the   edge   and   sky

white   after   white

all   day   long

light   leaves   the   ridge

as   long   as   light

is   all   that's   left

west   wind   and   cloud

then   moon   and   snow

all   one   way

along   the   ridge

two canyons

I.

cloud   and   earth   and

river   and   cloud

red   river   red   river

run

red   river   and   white   bone

chasm   and   cloud

the   cloud   and   its   shadow

red   river   and   rain

red   clouds   and   rain   shadow

gray   clouds   and   red   rain

the   canyon   above   and

white   bone   again

in   canyon   and   cloud

the   chord   and   its   shadow

red   river   red   river

run

2.

a   one

high   thing

wall   runs

and   to

a   an

long   other

water   one

falls   thing

from   runs

a   to

high   ground

gray   over

wall······and

above·····over

the········to

···········an

canyon····other

behind·····a

the········wall

high·······of

wall·······water

still······still

waters·····runs

run   to

a   an

ground other

a   some

high   where

hard   a

cloud   dry

in   wash

the

canyon some

     where

over   a

it   dead

all   end

one   hard

thing   high

runs   wall

to   the

an   dry

other   dead

          end

over   of

a   a

ground place

promontory

to   a
point

the   rock
runs   out

you   walk
and   point

to   the
rock

green   sky
above

green   river
below

where   it
all   ends

the   rock
and   you

run   out
of   it   all

brush
fires

1.

from
ridge
to
ridge

black
ash
and
cloud

fire
draws
a
line

2.

black
dawn
and
dusk

red
line
tonight

and
all
around

red
fire
above

3.

white
ash
above

black
ash
below

barbed
wire
between

fire
draws
a
line

4.

red

eyes

red

moon

a

cloud

and

light

red

eyes

red

moon

and

fire

all

night

5.

low
clouds
low
flame

a
fence
of
rain

the
black
wet
ground

and
ashes
ashes

all
fall
down

sunset

a

level

road

a

level

plain

a

level

bridge

and

all

below

the

level

black

fibonacci series

block   to

a   block

nother   a

box   and

stack   a

nother   to

a   mesa

nother   a

box   and

a   canyon

block   to

a   nother

red   and

a   black

nother   a

box   to

first   a

zero   then

a   one

nother   a

sum   of

sum   one

to   a

nother   a

black   to

block   a

nother   to

one   way

we   fold

stack   a

nother   to

a   way

fold   and

a   land

to   a

nother   to

stack   a

and   block

two   and

a   nother

a   zero

mesa   to

a   one

block   a

the winter field

I.

a   field   by   degrees
larger   than   vision

a   field   of   stones   and
snow   and   light

this   zero   field
sum   and   null

flat   light   and   stone
this   field   of   snow

2.

the   steel   and
carbon   sky

the   plate   steel   clouds
and   cracked   stone   sky

the   carbon   snow
its   weight   and   dates

the   copied   snow
the   cracked   ground

the   steel   and
carbon   ground

3.

the   empty   line   of
land   and   sky

gray   land   and
sky   and   a   cross

a   line   and   a
cross   of   white

the   empty   cross
and   its   line   of   sight

land   and   sky   all
in   a   line

all   across   the
gray   and   white

4.

the   steel   sky
and   the   white   cross
and   the   black   river

carbons   the   sky   the
ground   the   black
still   river

the   zero   river
sum   and   end

river   of   stone   and
still   light   across
the   winter   field

the inland sea

There is no sense of order that doesn't exist in nature.

MICHAEL HEIZER

I.

and   still   the   waves   pile   up   . . .   the
inland   sea   in   all   its   dry   tides   . . .
blank   shoreline   buried   and   reburied   every
night   beneath   . . .   long   lines   of
sand   and   shadow   . . .

the   desert   rises   and   falls   in   the   wind
. . .   sand   folds   up   and   falls   upon   . .
.   the   edge   of   the   dunes   . . .   against
the   long   division   of   basin   and   range   .
. .

sand   writes   at   right   angles   to   wind   . .
.   erasure   prevailing   from   west   to   east
. . .   and   in   retreat   before   the   wind   .
. .   your   footsteps   . . .   over   and   over
the   shoreline   again   . . .

2.

you rise and fall over the dunes . . .
walking at right angles to the edge .
. . horizon first above . . . then
below you . . . a sentence you carry
out from the interior . . . bearing
the long line of an old text . . .
rolled out of the ocean . . .

there is and is not . . . ocean in
the wind . . . and still the waves pile
up . . . meaning long since evaporated
. . . you and the dunes falling upon .
. . the edge of all you read . . .
stranded on a plain of salt . . .

the horizon . . . after all . . . comes
to an end . . . the shoreline disappears
. . . erasure intersects your path on an
old map . . . waves at right angles
to all you know . . . filling your
footsteps . . . one less line.

3.

sand   does   not   add   up   . . .   the   wind
the   water   . . .   shadows   yet   to   form
. . .   across   the   desert   floor   . . .

say   that   . . .   while   lying   on   your
back   . . .   on   top   of   the   largest   dune
. . .   sand   blowing   counter   clockwise
over   you   . . .   sand   piling   up   your
left   side   and   . . .   running   out   from
underneath   your   right   . . .

say   that   you   are   there   . . .   to   count
the   clouds   . . .   all   five   of   them
almost   over   the   horizon   . . .   and   by
adding   them   . . .   wish   to   derive the
weight   of   sunlight   . . .   at   this   end   of
the   valley   . . .

this   would   . . .   dictate   the   speed   of
the   wind   . . .   the   rate   at   which   . . .
you   are   at   once   buried   and   . . .
undermined   . . .   would   recall   the   tide   .
. .   where   once   the   waves   . . .   if   you
had   stood   at   the   edge   . . .   the
folding   unfolding   and   falling   edge   . . .
of   the   water

. . . would have undermined your weight . . . sinking you slowly into the shoreline . . . that line now depositing along your left side . . . feet facing the sun . . . which sinks of its own weight . . . behind the clouds . . .

4.

wind water and sand . . . do not yet add up to . . . the shadows unfolding here . . . from the mountains to the west . . . behind which the clouds . . . are now folding up the sun . . .

wind falls off . . . you roll down the crest of the dune . . . into its shadow . . . the cold shadow which does not yet . . . add up to the edge of . . . all you know . . . although it is close.

perforated object

for Robert F. & Michael Heizer

Flat perforated horn "pendant."—No. 43775 is a horn plate only 2 mm. thick. One end is rounded, the other squared. It is 120 mm. long and 45 mm. wide and has 90 holes, 5 mm. in diameter, drilled through it. It is very delicate and could be of little utilitarian value. It is perhaps a pendant used as a decoration.

(Robert F. Heizer, 1956)

Humboldt Cave . . . dates from about 2,000 years ago. It contained 31 cache pits and yielded a rich assemblage of specialized artifacts. Among them were sickles made of mountain sheep horn, bone awls, drills, fishhooks strung on lines, bundles of feathers, olivella shell beads, bone whistles, stone pipes, dart and arrow shafts, obsidian points, cottonwood bowls, string aprons and many other items. A shaman's kit consisting of articles for making magic and 766 pieces of coiled basketry were unearthed. (Samuel G. Houghton, 1976)

1.   The north star in one hole
          the rest all black—or held

          at arm's length during the day
          blue sky in every hole—or

5.   buried in sand and then picked up
          the ground flows through.

          Held in the hand
          fingering the holes
          what's empty of bone and sand

10.   and at once memory emerges.

The impression we got during the excavation of Humboldt Cave was that it served primarily as the equivalent of a safe-deposit box and secondarily as a retreat in time of necessity. That is not to say that the cave was not lived in, but we consider that there is no evidence of continuous occupation over long periods of time. (Heizer)

Set on edge in a high wind
one note of empty air

held up to the ear
whistle of an empty shore

15.   the inland sea
long blown away.

From the other side
through all the holes

one mirage

20.   very carefully—in all the holes
—all one cloud.

From the nature of the Humboldt Cave deposits and the fact that
the site lies four miles from water it would appear that the cave
served mainly as a temporary retreat, possibly in times of extreme
cold weather or war. A few fire pits and ash lenses were noted in
the deposits. The numerous caches of personal possessions seems
to argue against the probability of intensive and continuous oc-
cupation. (Heizer)

From this hole to that
fingering a line

one mountain to another
25.   a waterhole at a time.

A hole in the horn
for a year of life

counting off heat
counting off snow

30.   —days of birds
days of fish—

lining up the year.

Throughout the archeological continuum we find abundant evidence that fish, waterfowl, seeds, and water plants were the primary subsistence items. Some desert animals—mice, squirrels, antelope, deer, and mountain sheep—were obtained, but hunting seems to have been only an occasional pursuit. Rabbit hunting is a possible exception. (Heizer)

Drilling all day the
shape of night

35.   drilling all night
the sound of heat

take away as much as you can
take away until it breaks.

The bushes the geese the
40.   fish to be counted

the rain and sun and
wind to be counted

only one hole each
for each who lives here

45.   and no more.

The shaman, or medicine man . . . sometimes employed quite elaborate forms, using such aids as the Tsimshian soul-catcher (made of horn and abalone shell), the spirit whistle, the charm necklace, and other figures whose purposes have not in all cases been deciphered. (Houghton)

                One hole falls
                out of another

                order falls out of nothing
                lightning in every hole

50.   each hole a voice
                from the other side

                one hole one voice
                for each of the dead.

                At daybreak the lightning
55.   the thunder and memory

this many people

—and no more.

Tule, rushes, willow, and greasewood were the main materials
utilized for string, rope, baskets, clothing, and household ob-
jects. Aside from stone metates, mortars, sinkers, chipped
implements (points, knives, scrapers), a few ceremonial objects,
and a limited use of bone, the material culture is predominantly
based on perishable substances. Here are the unique prehistoric
materials to illustrate the amazingly efficient utilization of a
meager and forbidding environment. (Heizer)

Make one hole then another

until the last one breaks.

60.   walk this far

—then farther—

until the last one breaks.

All you know fits through

one thing at a time

65.   one hole at a time.

Held in the hand the far edge

so many holes
through which to fall.

The marshes were miles in extent and almost entirely covered by a
dense growth of tule, except where the river meandered through,
now and then expanding into a small lake. These marshes were
surrounded by a bare plain, consisting in the winter season of
mud, but at this time baked perfectly dry and hard by the heat of
the sun, except in the more depressed portions which were cov-
ered by a deep deposit of snow white "alkali." (Robert Ridgeway,
1877)

Planted on a stick—eye
70.   level from hole to horizon

—first the sun goes
down this hole
next day in the next.

All things grow cold until
75.   that—too—stops.

Planted on a stick

eyelevel with the morning sun

first in this hole then the next

the stick begins to grow.

From these extensive flats, desert plains lead away to the barren
mountains on either side, whose summits are bare and rugged
eruptive rocks, of weird forms and strange colors. Upon the
whole, the entire region was one of the most desolate and forbid-
ding that could be imagined. (Ridgeway)

80.   Dropped on the lake
                         the waves pass through—or

                         worn on a thong
                         around your neck

                         holes in the bone holes
85.   in the heart.

People pass through

one at a time

everyone leaves

and leaves behind

90.   a hole out of time.

Humboldt Lake . . . is now only a wind-swept playa over the
scoured surface of which sand dunes slowly migrate. (Heizer)

glass

What begins as undifferentiated space becomes place as we get to know it better and endow it with value. . . . Furthermore, if we think of space as that which allows movement, then place is pause; each pause in movement makes it possible for location to be transformed into place.

YI-FU TUAN

Place is material, material is place

MICHAEL HEIZER

archaeologos

I.

one   stone
to   the   next
lifted   up
and   out

inside   one
stone   the
wall

inside   the
next   a
room

inside   one
stone   the
present

inside   one
other   the
past

one
at   a   time
to   another

2.

one   room
to   the
next   room

door   to
door   the
past

the   only
roof   at
night

3.

from   this
stone   to
that   you
can   see
from   here
to   there

you   can
walk   from
this   stone
to   there

all   night
from   here
to   that
stone

one   time
to   the
next

4.

lift   it   up
one   stone

lift   it
up   and   a
line   runs

from   here   to
the   edge

all   night   the
line   worn
down   in
stone

5.

stone   by
still   stone
the   shadow
of   water

worn   down
by   water
a   shadow
in   stone

the   line
a   still   line
from   here   to
the   edge

worn   down
to   the   present
a   line
of   water

6.

from   here
to   there
this   line
worn   down
stone   to
stone

walking   at
night   every
where   at
a   time

new sand

1.

from   the   east
every   day
more   sand

white   wind
at   the   window

2.

sand   builds
its   house

day   by   day
next   to   ours

back   to   back

3.

wind   carries   sand
the   singing

the   empty   singing
into   the   city

wind   and   white
singing   dropped
at   the   edge

the   edge   of   the   wind
at   the   window

4.

wind   carries
the   silence   the

wind   carries
silence   the

the   silence
dropped   at   the

the   edge   of
the   wind   when
it   stops

pack   rats

I.

one   stick
one   stick
one   stick

at   a   time
one   stick
one   stick
at   a   time

one   here
and   then
one   there

from   here
to   there

one   piece
one   piece

to   there   one
at   a   time

2.

one   angle
one   angle
one   angle

at   a
time   one

angle   at
an   angle
one   angle

here   one
angle   there

one   angle
at   a   time

3.

this   piece
over   that
this   stick
over   that
this   stone
over   that

this   seed
over   that
this   stick
over   that
this   bone
over   that

this   stick
over   that
this   day
over   that

4.

from   one
rock   to
another

one   stick
from   one
rock   to

another
stick
and   in
between

sticks   upon
stones   from

one   rock

to

another

city

1.

in   the   shadow

in   the   shadow
of   the   valley

in   the   long   shadow
of   the   valley
airplanes

in   the   shadow
of   airplanes

in   the   shadow
of   airplanes   the
long   valley

in   the   long
valley   the   shadow
of   a   pit

a   shallow   pit
in   the   valley
of   airplanes

2.

above   the   shadow
of   the   pit   in
the   long   valley

above   the   pit
a   long   city
of   earth

in   the   shadow
of   airplanes

a   lone   city
of   earth

in   the   shadow
of   the   pit
airplanes

in   the   long
shadows
of   the   city

petroglyphs

1. *equinox*

in   the   rock
a   deep   line

and   across
the   rock
sunlight

and   deep
in   the   line
sunlight

hour   by   hour
sunlight
in   the   rock

and   across
the   deep
deep   land

a   long   line
of   rocks

2. *tinaja*

in   the   rock
shadows   in
the   red   rock

long   arms
and   snakes
shadows   in
the   rock

deep   in   the
rock   water
deep   water

arms   and
snakes
under   the   water

in   deep
shadow   the
red   shadow
of   arms   and
snakes

deep   water
and   rock

pictographs

1. *equinox*

across   the   rock
a   red   line
on   a   red   rock
a   red   line

across   the   red
rock   a   shadow
a   straight
shadow   falls

on   a   red
line   spring
crosses   into
summer

2.

red   line
red   rock
sun   and
dark   time

red   rock
dark   sun
short   lines
on   time

far   out
of   reach
far   over
head

red   lines
red   rock
dark   time
between

3. *fences*

red   rock
and   sand
black   lines
on   hand

black   lines
black   lines
from   rock
to   sand

red   sand
red   sand
long   lines
of   bone

scroll

for Mark Klett

I.

walking

    in

    the

    narrow

the

narrow

    rows

    of

    stone

    the

    stairs

    of

    sand

    stone

2.

from

rim

to

rim

rising

    over

    the

    rim

    the

    sun

    and

    the

    walking

3.

the canyon

    rises

    and

    falls

    in

    sunlight

a sand

world

risen

in stone

4.

walking

    the

    rim

    the

    sun

    walks

    down

    in

    time

falling

    down

    the

    rose

    walls

    of

    sand

    stone

time

    falls

    down

    the

    stairs

    of

    sand

    stone

time

    walking

    on

    the

    land

5.

in one
hand the
scroll

in the
other
the scroll

your eyes
in between
opening and
closing

walking from
left to
right

across the
top
of the text

6.

your hand
on the rock
trailing

one hand to
the other
over
all it sees

and the
country
rolls and
unrolls

a scroll
passed from
the time

of this
hand to
the time
of that.

disowning

I.

go   to   the   desert
lie   down   on
what   the   map
would   show   to
be   a   line

pick   yourself   up
find   another   line
lie   down
get   up

erase   all   the
lines   this   way
and   that

think   of   it   as
a   poem   without
line   without
lines   between

lines

think   of   it   as
picking   up
a   lie

2.

train your eyes
on the horizon
of the page

walk away from
it and every
thing else

train your eyes
to look down to
where words
fall away
beneath you

run your finger
down the page
and away from
the horizon

your eye follows
the finger the
horizon follows
your eyes

3.

stop   to   look
around   now
and   then   to
take   back   what
you   said

the   names
on   all   the
peaks   and
valleys

the   small
burrows
and   thin
shrubs
burning
on   the   desert
floor

pick   up   after
yourself   and
the   shadow   of
others   who
departed
before   you

the   loose
punctuation
blowing   by
in   the   wind

4.

a   blank   page

think   of   a   blank
page   at   the
end   of   a   book

closing   the   book
and   picking   up
your   steps   as

backwards
you   go

closing   up
the   mountains
and   sand   as
you   walk   off
the   land   and   out
of   the   words.

monody: a lyric ode sung by a single voice; a poem in which a mourner bewails someone's death; music in which the melody is confined to a single part; a monotonous sound. Theodore Monod, a French explorer of the Sahara.

geograph: a delineation or systematic arrangement of constituent elements.

"leaving elko," which memorializes the drive on Interstate 80 west from Elko to Winnemucca, was originally dedicated to Joann Serpa.

"two canyons" derives from flights made by Beth Fox over the Grand Canyon and the Rio Grande Gorge, and was dedicated to her.

"promontory"—White Rock Overlook, New Mexico.

"sunset" was written in memory of William Stafford while driving over the Rio Grande Gorge outside of Taos.

"fibonnaci series" was inspired by the drawings of Verne Stanford and dedicated to him; both the drawings and the poem are based on the architecture of Acoma Pueblo, New Mexico.

"the inland sea": Sand Mountain, Nevada, is a five-hundred-foot-high, mile-long sand dune located twenty-six miles east of Fallon.

"perforated object": Dr. Robert F. Heizer, the pre-eminent American anthropologist, excavated the Humboldt Cave in central Nevada during the summer of 1936, where he uncovered the "flat perforated 'horn' pendant." His son, the artist Michael Heizer, scaled up this "perforated object" into a sculpture measuring 27' long by 9'9" high and approximately 3'4" wide. The two-ton steel piece was installed in front of the Federal Courthouse in Reno, Nevada, in October 1996.

Heizer, Robert F., and Alex D. Krieger. "The Archaeology of Humboldt Cave, Churchill County, Nevada" (Berkeley: University of California Press, 1956).

Ridgeway, Robert. "U.S. Geological Exploration of the Fortieth Parallel," as quoted by Heizer.

Houghton, Samuel G. *A Trace of Desert Waters* (Reno: University of Nevada Press, 1976).

glass: a material, usually transparent, created by fusing sand.

"pack rats" derives from a series of photographs taken over several decades by Michael Heizer of pack rat middens.

"city" is in homage to the very large sculpture of the same name, which Michael Heizer has been working on in eastern central Nevada since 1971. Its initial elements consisted of huge berms surrounding a deep pit into which several concrete forms have been integrated. The site is a favorite of the U.S. military for flyovers.

petroglyph is art carved into a rock; *pictograph* is art painted on a rock. Both of these are from Lincoln County in eastern central Nevada and not far from *city*.

tinajas are naturally eroded potholes most often occurring atop large rock surfaces. Holding water and occasionally topped with rocks trimmed to fit tightly and prevent evaporation, their presence is sometimes noted by rock art nearby.

fences was how Dr. Heizer described those examples of rock art that consist of long horizontal lines with short tick marks extending downward. He hypothesized in the 1960s that the marks signified where hunters should build brush- and stoneworks in order to channel animals into a trap where they could be killed with spears, throwing sticks (*atlatls*), or arrows. Contemporary anthropologists surmise that they mark the summer/winter solstices, and the spring/autumnal equinoxes. Neither is conclusively proven, though evidence favors the latter.

scroll: The noted American photographer Mark Klett, with whom I have collaborated for several years, took a team of us one night to his favorite camping spot shown him years earlier by Edward Abbey. Muley Point, a series of long sandstone ledges, hangs over the San Juan River and looks into Monument Valley. The recursiveness of the landscape we witnessed upon waking the next morning was not only the corollary to these poems but pointed as well to a new way of assembling the series of photographs that Klett was beginning to refer to as a scroll.

The composer Steve Reich is quoted from his essay "Music as a Gradual Process," which appeared in *Writings About Music* (New York: New York University Press, 1974).

Quotes by Michael Heizer are from the exhibition catalog edited by Julia Brown, *Michael Heizer: Sculpture in Reverse* (Los Angeles: Museum of Contemporary Art, 1984).

The quote by Yi-Fu Tuan is from his *Space and Place: The Perspective of Experience* (Minneapolis: University of Minnesota Press, 1977).

The words of Edmond Jabés that appear at the beginning and end are taken out of an interview with Marcel Cohen that appears in *From the Desert to the Book* (Barrytown, N.Y.: Station Hill Press, 1980).

As far as the word desert *is concerned, what fascinates me is to see how far the metaphor of the void, from being used so much, has permeated the whole word. The word itself has become a metaphor. To give it back its strength, one has therefore to return to the real desert which is indeed exemplary emptiness—but emptiness with its own, very real dust. Think also about the word* book. *The book, where everything seems possible through a language that one thinks one can master and that finally turns out to be but the very place of its bankruptcy. All the metaphors the word can inspire lie between these two extremes. None of them really gets to the heart of it, but between this all and this nothing, the unfathomable opening takes place, which in the end is what every writer and every reader is confronted with.*

EDMOND JABÉS

BETH FOX

William L. Fox is the author of six nonfiction books on the cultural geography of the American Southwest, more than a dozen books of poetry, and is currently at work on a book about scientific and artistic images of the Antarctic. His poems have appeared in more than 60 magazines and journals, and he edited the *West Coast Poetry Review* for many years. He is the Western States Arts Federation literature consultant.